The secret history o

The Czech Connection

COMPILED BY NEIL REES

The Czechoslovak Government in Exile in London and Buckinghamshire during the Second World War

Pre-war Czechoslovak full coat of arms with Bohemian lions as bearers, lime tree leaves and the national motto "Pravda vítězí" (Truth Prevails).

First published in Great Britain 2005 by Neil Rees as a limited edition of 1,500 copies.

ISBN 0-9550883-0-5

Typeset by Hawkes Design, Chesham, Buckinghamshire, England

Printed by Croxsons, Chesham, Buckinghamshire, England

Contact: Neil Rees, 1 Eskdale Avenue, Chesham, Buckinghamshire, HP5 3AX, England
www.czechsinexile.org e-mail: neil.rees@czechsinexile.org
The author welcomes correspondence. Any corrections or new information can be included in future editions.

INTRODUCTION

I was born in Aylesbury, Buckinghamshire (Bucks), in the south-east of England. In the 1970s and 1980s I frequently visited my grandmother in the hamlet of Rowsham, near Aylesbury, down the road from a bus shelter donated to the villages of Aston Abbotts and Wingrave by the President of Czechoslovakia. Like most people who pass it, I never thought of its significance.

In 1990 I went to teach English in Czechoslovakia. Whilst there I was befriended by some British war brides. They told me the story of how they had married Czechoslovak soldiers in exile in Britain during the war; how in 1945 they went to live in Czechoslovakia, and how they were trapped by communism from 1948 until 1989.

Looking at second-hand bookshops in Prague, I was amazed to find photographs of Buckinghamshire in many wartime and pre-communist books. So I started to collect them.

When Czech and Slovak friends have come to visit me in Bucks I have been in the habit of taking them to Aston Abbotts. I would show them where their President lived during the war and the bus shelter he left. My friends would ask me questions about the local Czech connection that I could not answer – so I decided to investigate.

Under communism Czechs and Slovaks had been taught that the Czechoslovak government was in exile in London. This was true, but talking to locals around Bucks and Beds I found a fascinating untold story of the President of Czechoslovakia at Aston Abbotts, the officials of his private office at Wingrave, his military intelligence staff at Addington and a military intelligence radio station at Hockliffe.

This book is the fruit of my research. It uses pictures from archives in Prague and items kindly lent to me by people I have met. Where possible I have used the photographers' original captions; otherwise, information is from the memories and writings of people who were there.

This is the secret story of the Czechoslovak Government in Exile in London, and how three small Buckinghamshire villages became sanctuary to the President of Czechoslovakia and his officials from 1940 until 1945.

Neil Rees, Buckinghamshire, England, May 2005

4. Aston Abbotts, Bucks, July 2004   Photo by NEIL REES

THE CZECHOSLOVAK CONNECTION CHRONOLOGY

FOUNDATION OF CZECHOSLOVAKIA

28 October	1918	Czechoslovakia declares independence from Austro-Hungary
11 November	1918	Armistice Day: end of the First World War
14 November	1918	Tomáš Masaryk becomes 1st Czechoslovak President
1 June	1925	Jan Masaryk becomes Ambassador in London

THE COUNTDOWN TO WAR

30 January	1933	Adolf Hitler comes to power in Germany
18 December	1935	Dr Edvard Beneš becomes 2nd Czechoslovak President
29 September	1938	Munich Agreement: Sudetenland ceded to Germany
5 October	1938	German troops annex Sudetenland, Beneš resigns
22 October	1938	Dr Beneš goes into exile and moves to Putney, London
14 March	1939	Declaration of independent Slovakia under Josef Tiso
15 March	1939	Germany declares Protectorate of Bohemia-Moravia
1 September	1939	Germany invades Poland
3 September	1939	Great Britain declares war on Germany

THE SECOND WORLD WAR

10 May	1940	Winston Churchill becomes British Prime Minister
22 June	1940	Capitulation of France
9 July	1940	Edvard Beneš becomes President-in-Exile in London
22 July	1940	Churchill sets up the Special Operations Executive (SOE)
18 August	1940	Start of the Battle of Britain and the London Blitz
13 November	1940	Beneš and his presidential guards arrive at Aston Abbotts
18 July	1941	Churchill fully recognises Beneš's Government-in-Exile
6 December	1941	Japan attacks Pearl Harbor: USA enters the war

CZECHOSLOVAK EVENTS

27 May	1942	Assassination of Reinhard Heydrich in Prague
10 June	1942	Nazis destroy the village of Lidice in Bohemia
5 August	1942	British government revokes the Munich Agreement

EVENTS IN BUCKINGHAMSHIRE

24 December	1942	Dr Beneš gives globe to Aston Abbotts School
28 October	1943	Jubilee lime tree planted at The Abbey, Aston Abbotts
15 April	1944	Beneš gives bus shelter to Wingrave and Aston Abbotts

THE COUNTDOWN TO VICTORY

6 June	1944	D-Day landings in Normandy
29 August	1944	Slovak Uprising begins
11 March	1945	Czechoslovak Government-in-Exile flies to Moscow
4 April	1945	New Czechoslovak Government set up in Košice, Slovakia
5 May	1945	Prague Uprising begins
8 May	1945	V.E. Day: Germany surrenders - Victory in Europe

RESTORATION OF DEMOCRATIC CZECHOSLOVAKIA

9 May	1945	Red Army troops enter Prague
16 May	1945	Czechoslovak Government returns to Prague
26 May	1946	Dr Edvard Beneš re-elected as Czechoslovak President
27 February	1948	Communist coup in Prague

COMMUNIST CZECHOSLOVAKIA

10 March	1948	Jan Masaryk found dead in Prague aged 61
7 June	1948	President Beneš resigns
3 September	1948	President Beneš dies at Sezimovo Ústí aged 64
21 August	1968	Soviet-led troops invade Czechoslovakia
2 December	1974	Mrs Hana Beneš dies at Sezimovo Ústí aged 89
9 November	1989	Berlin Wall starts to come down
17 November	1989	Velvet Revolution: end of communism in Prague

POST-COMMUNIST EUROPE

29 December	1989	Václav Havel becomes President of Czechoslovakia
30 June	1991	Last Soviet-led troops leave Czechoslovakia
1 January	1993	Velvet Divorce: Czechoslovakia splits into two states
20 October	1998	Václav Havel visits Wingrave and Aston Abbotts
1 May	2004	Czech & Slovak Republics join the European Union (EU)
1 May	2005	Lidice roses and lime tree planted at Aston Abbotts

Great Britain

Czech Republic

Slovak Republic

5. Jan Masaryk (1886-1948)

Jan Garrigue Masaryk was the only surviving son of Tomáš Garrigue Masaryk, the first President of Czechoslovakia. He was divorced and had no children of his own. Jan was appointed Czechoslovak Minister to the Court of St. James (Ambassador) in 1925, and kept a flat at 58 Westminster Gardens, London. Between 1939 and 1945 he made a weekly BBC broadcast called *Volá Londýn* (London Calling).

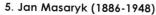

Photo taken in London by ERICH AUERBACH. Information courtesy of DR DAGMAR HÁJKOVÁ

6. Dr Edvard Beneš (1884-1948)

In this photograph Tomáš Masaryk is shown in the framed portrait behind Dr Beneš. President Masaryk resigned due to ill-health in 1935, and Dr Edvard Beneš became the Second President on 18th December 1935. Dr Beneš was President when Adolf Hitler rose to power in Germany.

Photo taken in Aston Abbotts by ERICH AUERBACH

7. President Edvard Beneš of Czechoslovakia

On 29th September 1938 the Munich Agreement awarded Nazi Germany the majority German-speaking borderlands of Bohemia and Moravia, known as the Sudetenland. President Beneš resigned on 5th October 1938 when the Germans annexed the Sudetenland, and he went into exile to London.

Photo taken in London by ERICH AUERBACH, 1942

8. Beneš's house in Putney 1938-1940

On 22nd October 1938 President Beneš moved to Putney, London, where he had a nephew, Bohumil (Bohuš) Beneš (1901-1977), son of Václav Beneš. Dr Beneš lived at 26 Gwendolen Avenue, Putney, with his wife Hana and their nieces until November 1940, when German bombing during the Blitz made the area too dangerous for them to live in.

Photo taken in Putney on 28th October 1939 by ERICH AUERBACH

9. Plaque

This blue plaque was put on the house in 1978 by the Smutný family, who owned the house from 1950 to 1979.

Photo by NEIL REES, 2004

10. & 11. Patriotic labels

Propaganda 'V' for Victory labels issued in 1941.

Courtesy of PIERS PETTMAN

12. Czechoslovaks in exile

Germany invaded the Czech lands of Bohemia and Moravia on 15th March 1939. About 20,000 Czechoslovak refugees came to Britain. President Beneš formed land and air forces in France and then the UK, and set up a Government in Exile, working with Winston Churchill and the Allies.

Courtesy of BERNARD OSBORN from a philatelic folder

13. Beneš's offices in London, 1939-1940

President Beneš's original London offices were at 114-116 Park Street. Shortly after this photograph was taken in April 1940, the building was destroyed by German bombing during the Blitz. President Beneš's office then moved to 9 Grosvenor Place, London until March 1945.

Photo by ERICH AUERBACH. Signed copy courtesy of MIROSLAV SMUTNÝ

14. Winston Churchill poster

Translation of poster text: *"Czechoslovaks! The hour of your liberation is coming!"* From his Buckinghamshire base at Chequers, British Prime Minister Winston Churchill worked with the Czechoslovaks and other Allies for the liberation of Nazi-occupied Europe.

Courtesy of the family of JAROSLAV BUBLÍK

15. Jan Masaryk, Czechoslovak Ambassador

Jan Masaryk had been Czechoslovak Ambassador to London since 1st June 1925. He was a very popular character. Amongst his British friends were Bruce Lockhart (1887-1970), a former agent in Russia who spoke Russian and Czech; and Anthony de Rothschild, whose family had business connections in Czechoslovakia.

Photo taken 1943 in London by ERICH AUERBACH

16. Ascott House, Ascott, near Wing, Buckinghamshire

Ascott House was home to Anthony (1887-1961) and Yvonne de Rothschild (1899-1977), and their children. Jan Masaryk was a frequent guest at weekends, or for Sunday lunch, coming with his black Scottie dog. Other visitors included Bruce Lockhart and President Beneš. Anthony de Rothschild used his local connections in the Whaddon Chase Hunt to find safe country residences in Buckinghamshire for his Czechoslovak friends.

Photo from author's collection. Information courtesy of RENÉE ROBESON. Ascott House is now a National Trust property

Rex Leeper   President Beneš   Hugh Dalton   Bruce Lockhart

17. Arrival in Bucks

President Beneš arrived at The Abbey, Aston Abbotts on 13th November 1940.

He was welcomed by a delegation from the British Special Operations Executive (SOE), who were based nearby at Woburn, Bedfordshire.

Left to right:
Reginald (Rex) Leeper (1917-1968), Director of the Political Warfare Executive (PWE);

President Beneš;

Hugh Dalton (1887-1962), Minister for Economic Warfare and responsible for the SOE;

Bruce Lockhart, liaison officer to the Czechoslovak Government-in-exile.

18. The Gatehouse, Aston Abbotts

The gateway and gatehouse Lodge to The Abbey; photograph taken from the Green.

Courtesy of PETER KENT

19. Parish Church of St James, Aston Abbotts

The Church dates back to the 13th century. During the war it held church parades for the Czechoslovak guards.

Photo courtesy of PETER KENT. Information courtesy of COLIN HIGGS

20. Aston Abbotts postmark

Village Post Office frank.

Courtesy of BERNARD OSBORN

21. The Green, Aston Abbotts

Picture of the Green at Aston Abbotts showing the signpost.

Courtesy of PETER KENT

22. Bucks County

Top of the signpost.

Photo 2005 by NEIL REES

23. Coming up the driveway
One of the gardeners, Charlie Griffin, coming up the drive to The Abbey on his bicycle.

Courtesy of the MASARYK INSTITUTE, Prague. Information courtesy of VICTOR SCOTT

25. Bucks badge
The white swan on a red and black shield is the emblem of the historic county of Buckinghamshire.

JOURNEY TO LONDON
Aston Abbotts is 40 miles to the north of central London. During the war the journey took 1½ hours by car

24. Front entrance to The Abbey
Entrance gate to The Abbey. A Czechoslovak soldier was on guard whenever the President was at home.

Courtesy of the MASARYK INSTITUTE, Prague

26. Back entrance to The Abbey
Jan Filip & Josef Hodek (front) walking from The Abbey.

Photo and information courtesy of HILDA HARPER

27. Leaving Aston Abbotts for London
President Beneš would leave in his Daimler at 8:30 a.m.

Photo from 28th October 1941 courtesy of the MILITARY ARCHIVE, Prague

28. The President's Library

Original caption: *"The President of the Czechoslovak Republic going through part of his extensive library at his Buckinghamshire home."*

Photo and caption by ERICH AUERBACH

29. The President's Books

At The Abbey in Aston Abbotts President Beneš had a large collection of books in English, French, Czech, Russian and German. His daily English newspapers were delivered by George Brandon.

Photo by ERICH AUERBACH

30. President's Aston Abbotts Office

President Beneš converted the billiards room of The Abbey into his office. He worked from Aston Abbotts on Mondays, in the evenings, at weekends, or when he had no appointments in London. As the war progressed, he spent more time at Aston Abbotts.

Photo by ERICH AUERBACH

31. President's Desk

Original caption: *"The working desk of the President of the Republic at his Buckinghamshire home."*

Photo and caption by ERICH AUERBACH

THE ABBEY, ASTON ABBOTTS, NEAR AYLESBURY, BUCKINGHAMSHIRE

The Abbey at Aston Abbotts is a primarily Georgian building built on the site of a former monastic abbey, which belonged to the abbots of St. Albans until 1534. The house belonged to the Morton family from 1924 to 1988. It is a private house and not open to the public.

32. Engraving of the President's country residence (front view)

In November 1940 President Beneš, his family and household staff moved out of Putney to escape the Blitz. They lived at The Abbey, Aston Abbotts until March 1945. It was leased for 20 guineas (£21) a week from Captain Harold Morton (1894-1972) and Mrs Beatrice Morton (1893-1988).

Engraving from 1942 by CAPTAIN JOSEF PODHORA, courtesy of MICHAL KOLÁŘ

33. Photograph of the President's country residence (rear view)

Aston Abbotts was President Beneš's headquarters for receiving British, Czechoslovak and other Allied officials, Ministers and Generals. At Aston Abbotts, Beneš wrote his books and speeches, and planned the resistance and liberation operations.

Photo taken in 1942 courtesy of the MILITARY ARCHIVE, Prague

34. Czechoslovak London Government-in-Exile Addresses 1938-1945

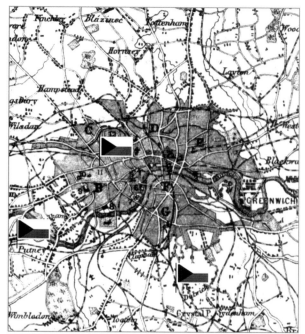

8 Grosvenor Place, London SW1	Czechoslovak Legation (Embassy) (since 1919)
58 Westminster Gardens, London	Jan Masaryk's private flat (1925-1948)
26 Gwendolen Avenue, Putney	President Beneš's residence (Oct 1938 - Nov 1940)
114 Park Street, London	President, Chancellery and Foreign Affairs (1939-1940)
Rosendale Road, West Dulwich	Military Intelligence services (March 1939 - May 1940)
Dukes Hill, Woldingham, Surrey	Military Intelligence radio station (May 1940 - Aug 1942)

London offices, Hyde Park area, 1940-1945

9 Grosvenor Place, SW1	Offices of President Beneš, Mrs Beneš & the Chancellery
23 Wilton Crescent, SW1	Military Chancellery Offices
43 Wilton Crescent, SW7	State Council Offices
62 Princes Gate, SW7	Prime Minister and Council of Ministers Office
62E Princes Gate, SW7	Ministry of the Interior
35 Cadogan Gardens, SW3	Ministry of Social Welfare
2 Wilton Crescent, SW1	Ministry of Education
134 Piccadilly, W1	Ministry of National Defence
15 Grosvenor Place, SW1	Inspectorate of the Air Force
Porchester Gate, Bayswater W2	Military Intelligence offices
Fursecroft, George St, SW1	Other government Ministries
35 Porchester Terrace, W2	Czechoslovak Red Cross
18 Grosvenor, Place, SW1	Czechoslovak Institute
54 Keswick Road, SW15	"Čechoslovák" publishers and bookshop

LONDÝN s OKOLÍM.
Měřítko 1 : 300.000.

Části města.
A.City. B.Westminster. C.Marylebone. D.Finsbury.
E.Tower Hamlets. F.Southwark. G.Lambeth.
Veřejné budovy a zahrady:
1. Banka a bursa.   5. S. James ský palác.   9. Palác výstavní.
2. Chrám S. Pavla.   6. Sněmovna.   10. Sady Kensingtonské.
3. Tower.   7. Vězení Milbankské.   11. Hyde Park.
4. Britské Museum.   8. Nemocnice Chelsea.   12. Regent Park.

Map of London published in Czech.
It was used by a Czech soldier from Tábor who was stationed in England during the war.

Information from: "Czechoslovak List", published by the Czechoslovak Ministry of Foreign Affairs, London, September 1944
Courtesy of MONICA BEAUMONT

35. President's London Office

President Beneš's Daimler outside
9 Grosvenor Place, where the President,
his wife and his officials had their offices.
They usually arrived from Aston Abbotts
at about 10 a.m. Their chauffeur was
Mr Sydney Byatt.

Photo taken 10th September 1941 by ERICH AUERBACH.

36. President's Offices, London, 1940-45

Original caption: *"The President of the
Czechoslovak Republic in conversation
with Dr Hubert Ripka (left), acting
Czechoslovak Foreign Minister and
Dr Smutný of the President's Chancellery.
(Picture taken in the Chancellery.)"*

Photo taken 16th October 1941 by ERICH AUERBACH

37. Returning to Aston Abbotts, Bucks

President Beneš left his London office most
days at about 6:30 p.m. As shown in this
picture, Dr Beneš was usually accompanied
by his wife (Mrs Hana Beneš) and her personal
secretary, their bodyguard (in uniform) and
Dr Edvard Táborský, Beneš's personal secretary.

Photo by ERICH AUERBACH[?]

President Beneš   Mrs Hana Beneš   Queen Elizabeth (1900-2002)

38. With the Queen

Original caption:

"*Queen Elizabeth visited the Hollar exhibition at the Czechoslovak Institute, London. Her Majesty who was met by the President of Czechoslovakia and Madam Beneš, examined with interest the works of Wenceslas Hollar, the famous Czech engraver who is buried at St. Margaret's, Westminster. Many of the exhibits have been lent by the King from the Royal collection at Windsor Castle.*"
23rd April 1942

Photo and caption by ERICH AUERBACH

CZECHOSLOVAK INSTITUTE

The Czechoslovak Institute at 18 Grosvenor Place, London was opened on 21st January 1941.
It was a Czechoslovak cultural centre and hosted exhibitions and talks.

39. Seat of the Czechoslovak Government-in-Exile

Original caption:

"Czechoslovak Government Headquarters. 'Fursecroft' at the corner of George Street-Brown Street, London, W.1. which houses the Ministries of Foreign Affairs including the Department of Information, Finance, Justice, Economic Reconstruction and the Czechoslovak Audit Bureau."

Photo and caption by ERICH AUERBACH, 1941

40. Government meeting

Meeting of the Czechoslovak Government-in-Exile Council of Ministers at their offices in 62 Princes Gate, Exhibition Road, London S.W.7. On the left is Jan Masaryk, Foreign Minister and Deputy Prime Minister. Behind him is Juraj Slávik, Minister of the Interior. At the head of the table is the Prime Minister, Monsignor Jan Šrámek, who chaired their meetings.

Photo by ERICH AUERBACH

41. Ministers of the Czechoslovak Government-in-Exile in London

Left to right: Dr Jaroslav Stránský (1884-1973), Minister of Justice; Dr Hubert Ripka (1895-1958), State Secretary for Foreign Affairs; Dr Edvard Outrata (1898-1958), Minister of Business and Commerce; Monsignor Jan Šrámek (1870-1956), Prime Minister; Ján Lichner (1897-1979), Minister of Argriculture; Ján Bečko (1889-1972), Minister of Social Welfare; Dr Edvard Beneš (1884-1948), President; František Němec (1898-1963), Minister for Economic Reconstruction; General Sergej Ján Ingr (1894-1956), Minister of Defence; Dr Ladislav Feierabend (1891-1969), Minister of Finance; Jan Masaryk (1886-1948), Minister of Foreign Affairs; General Rudolf Viest (1890-1945), Deputy Minister of Defence; Juraj Slávik (1890-1969), Minister of the Interior.

Photo taken at 9 Grosvenor Place, London, on Czechoslovak Independence Day (28th October), 1941 by ERICH AUERBACH

43. The Old Manor House, Wingrave, Buckinghamshire

Wingrave Manor was built by Hannah de Rothschild between 1876 and 1878.
It belonged to the Stewart-Freeman family from 1898 to 1972. Today the house and grounds belong to the MacIntyre Trust. They are not open to the public.

42. Residence of the President's officials at Wingrave

In November 1940 the President's officials moved out of London to escape the Blitz. They leased the Old Manor House from Mary Eveline Stewart-Freeman (1882-1955), Countess of Essex, for £20 a week.

Photos from 1946 courtesy of HARRODS

44. Czechoslovak officials at Wingrave

Left to right: Mr Leopold Matouš, the caretaker and major-domo of the Old Manor House at Wingrave; the visiting artist Mrs Hladiková[?]; Dr Jaromír Smutný, Chief of the President's Office; and General Oldřich Španiel, President Beneš's Military Adviser. These men lived at Wingrave. The House was also a hostel for visiting Czechoslovaks.

Photo taken in 1945 courtesy of the MASARYK INSTITUTE, Prague. Information courtesy of MIROSLAV SMUTNÝ

45. Czechoslovak national costume

Mrs Kathleen Hampson wearing her Czechoslovak friend's national costume. The picture is taken in her garden at Mill House Cottage, Wingrave.

Photo taken in 1943, courtesy of CHERRY-ANNE EVANS

47. Czech soldier

Picture drawn by Milan Smutný, eldest son of Jaromír Smutný. He was a soldier in the Artillery of the Czechoslovak Army and stayed in Wingrave when he was on leave.

Courtesy of PRUDENCE GOODWIN from a 1945 Christmas card

46. The guards' cook visiting Wingrave

The cook from the Aston Abbotts presidential guards sometimes came to Wingrave, where they kept pigs and rabbits.

Photo taken in 1945 courtesy of the MASARYK INSTITUTE, Prague

CZECHOSLOVAK CHANCELLERY OFFICIALS AT WINGRAVE

The Old Manor House at Wingrave was a residence for the staff and families of the President's Private Office (Chancellery), under Dr Jaromír Smutný (1892-1964); and the Military Office (Military Chancellery) under General Antonín Hasal (1883-1960) until 1944, and then under General Oldřich Španiel (1894-1963). Jan Masaryk also frequently stayed at Wingrave.

48. Arriving at Aston Abbotts

At Wingrave, the officials had two black Austin cars which they used to travel to their offices in London or for meetings at Aston Abbotts. Here Jaromír Smutný and General Oldřich Španiel arrive at Aston Abbotts.

Photo taken 1945 courtesy of the MASARYK INSTITUTE, Prague. Information courtesy of MIROSLAV SMUTNÝ

49. Meeting at Aston Abbotts

Original caption: *"The President of the Czechoslovak Republic at a tea time conversation with General Španiel and Dr Smutný, chief of the President's Chancellery."*

Photo and caption by ERICH AUERBACH, 1944

DR EDVARD TÁBORSKÝ (1910-1996)

Dr Edvard Táborský was President Beneš's personal secretary. He lived at Wingrave, but worked with President Beneš every day in London, or at Aston Abbotts. In October 1943 he married his colleague Miss Edith Calder. After the war, he became the Czechoslovak Ambassador to Sweden, and in 1948 he went to the United States of America and worked at The University of Texas at Austin, retiring as Professor Emeritus.

50. Military Map

Original caption: *"The President of the Czechoslovak Republic and his personal secretary Dr Edvard Táborský, studying the latest situation on a large scale map of Czechoslovakia."*

Photo and caption by ERICH AUERBACH, 1944

51. Dr Edvard Táborský

Original caption: *"Dr. Edvard Táborský, personal secretary reporting to the President of the Czechoslovak Republic in the study of Dr. Beneš's Buckinghamshire home."*

Photo and caption by ERICH AUERBACH, 1944

52. Chequers Court, Butler's Cross, near Ellesborough, Buckinghamshire

Chequers is a Tudor building which was updated in Victorian Gothic style. It was given to the nation in 1921 by Lord and Lady Lee of Farnham as a private country residence for the British Prime Minister. It is not open to the public.

53. Chequers

Between 1940 and 1945, British Prime Minister Winston Churchill used Chequers as his headquarters for conducting the war. Chequers is about 8 miles from Aston Abbotts, which was convenient for meetings between him and President Beneš.

Pictures from local postcards.

54. Mary Durasová (1898-1982)

Original caption: *"Mary Durasová, the well known sculptress, is working in her Buckinghamshire studio on a bust of the Prime Minister. Mrs. Durasová's hostess is Miss Augusta North, an English artist. As Mr. Churchill is too busy with the war, Mary Durasová had to model his head according to photographs. Here she is comparing work and photograph in her library."*

Photo and caption by ERICH AUERBACH, 1941

55. Winston Churchill inspecting Czechoslovak troops

On 19th April 1941, Winston Churchill inspected Czechoslovak Army troops at their bases near Leamington Spa. He was accompanied by President Beneš and members of the provisional Czechoslovak Government-in-Exile.

56. Tea with the Churchills, 20th April 1941

President Beneš *(centre)* took tea with Winston Churchill (1874-1965) and Mrs Clementine Churchill (1885-1977) and officers of the Czechoslovak Brigade at Moreton Paddox House near Warwick. As a result of this meeting, Winston Churchill fully recognised the provisional Czechoslovak Government-in-Exile on 18th July 1941, as the legitimate and future government of Czechoslovakia.

58. Addington House – The Military Intelligence residence

In 1940 the Czecholsovak Military Intelligence staff and their families moved out of West Dulwich, London, to escape the Blitz. The Czechoslovak families of Moravec, Strankmüller, Cigna and Fořt lived at Addington House with Major Harold Gibson, their British Secret Intelligence Services (SIS) liaison officer, until 1945.

57. Addington House, Addington, near Winslow, Buckinghamshire

A Queen Anne style building, near Winslow in Bucks. In the 1940s it belonged to Croxton C. B. Smith-Bingham. Today it is divided into 4 private dwellings and is not open to the public.

59. Christening at St Mary's Parish Church, Addington

The christening of John Jameson, son of Squadron Leader John Jameson and Mrs Mabel Jameson of Seven Gables, Addington on 16th April 1944. In the background are members of the British and Czechoslovak Intelligence Services who lived at Addington.

Photo courtesy of CYRIL CORBETT, 1944. Information courtesy of PATRICK HOUSE

CZECHOSLOVAK MILITARY RADIO STATIONS

The Czechoslovak Military Intelligence ran a wireless transmission station. Between 1940 and 1942 this was at Woldingham, Surrey, but in August 1942, the SOE set up a new station on a farm at Hockliffe, near Leighton Buzzard, Bedfordshire. This was supplied with equipment from the Special Communications Unit (SCU) at Whaddon Hall, Buckinghamshire.

60. Czechoslovak Military Intelligence staff group
Left to right: Col. František Moravec (1895-1966), head of Military Intelligence; Captain Jaroslav Tauer, treasurer; Major Harold Gibson; Captain Alois Čáslavka, assistant; President Beneš; Prokop Drtina, political adviser; Gen. Sergej Ingr; Dr Smutný.

61. Hockliffe Radio Station, Bedfordshire
Left to right: Václav Retich (1909-1980s), Captain Václav Knotek (1910-1948), Jan Štursa (1917-2000). The Station kept in contact with Czechoslovak embassies in neutral countries, the Czech resistance and paratroop mission radio operators. It had 10 permanent members under the command of Captain Zdeněk Gold.

62. Chicheley Hall, Chicheley, near Newport Pagnell, Buckinghamshire

Chicheley Hall was built in the Georgian style by Sir John Chester between 1719 and 1723. During the war Chicheley Hall was requisitioned by the SOE as a Special Training School (STS) number 46, for explosives and radio operations training for Allied paratroop missions. Today, Chicheley Hall is a conference centre.

63. Chicheley Hall – STS 46

STS 46 was used for training Czechoslovak paratroopers from 1942 to 1943. They then left Chicheley Hall to go on secret operations into Czechoslovakia.

Courtesy of BUCKS COUNTY MUSEUM, Aylesbury

64. Radio operations training

Radio operators were trained at Chicheley Hall and also at STS 52 Thame Park, Thame, Oxfordshire. Sergeant Lubomír Jasínek (1922-1943) *(centre)*, was the radio operator on Operation Antinomy in 1942.

Photo taken 1942 courtesy of the family of JAROSLAV BUBLÍK

OPERATION ANTHROPOID – ASSASSINATION OF REINHARD HEYDRICH 1942

The Czechoslovak Military Intelligence planned many paratroop missions into the German-occupied Protectorate of Bohemia-Moravia.
The most famous is Operation Anthropoid, the operation to assassinate the German Reichsprotektor Reinhard Heydrich (1904-1942). Jan Kubiš
(1913-1942) and Josef Gabčik (1912-1942) were trained by the SOE and flown out on 28th December 1941. They succeeded in attacking Heydrich
in Prague on 27th May 1942 and he died of his wounds. In retribution the Germans destroyed the Czech villages of Lidice and Ležáky in June
1942, killing most of the inhabitants. Heydrich's assassins were tracked down by the Germans to Prague Orthodox Church where they died on
18th June 1942. Lidice became a symbol of Nazi atrocities, and led Winston Churchill to revoke the Munich Agreement on 5th August 1942.

65. Military Discussion at Aston Abbotts
Left to right: General František Moravec (alias Musil), based at Addington;
President Beneš; and General Antonín Hasal (alias Nižborský), who was
Beneš's military adviser from 1940 until 1944, based at Wingrave.

Photo taken 1944 courtesy of the MASARYK INSTITUTE, Prague

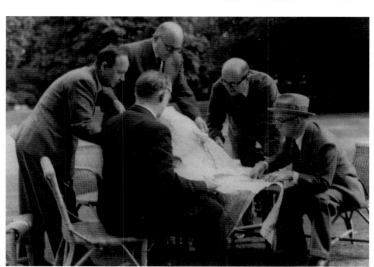

66. Military Planning at Aston Abbotts
Left to right: Rex Leeper, Director of the PWE, based at Woburn;
General František Moravec; Jaromír Smutný, Beneš's chief of staff;
Jan Masaryk; and President Beneš, looking at a map of the Front.

Photo courtesy of the MASARYK INSTITUTE, Prague

OTTO HELLER (1896-1970)

Otto Heller was a Czechoslovak film-maker who began his career filming the funeral of Austrian Emperor Franz Josef in November 1916. Amongst his later films were *The Ladykillers* in 1955, *Richard III* in 1955 and *Alfie* in 1966.

67. Film-maker at Aston Abbotts

Left to right:
Jan Masaryk; František Moravec; Rex Leeper; Bruce Lockhart; Otto Heller, (behind the camera); President Beneš; Jaromír Smutný

Courtesy of MICHAL KOLÁŘ

FILMS AT ASTON ABBOTTS

Events filmed at Aston Abbotts included: a speech by Beneš about the destruction of Lidice in 1942; the planting of a jubilee liberty lime tree on 31st October 1943, marking the 25th anniversary of the foundation of Czechoslovakia; and a film of President Beneš for his 60th birthday in May 1944.

ERICH AUERBACH (1911-1977)

Erich Auerbach was born at Falkenau (now Sokolov) in Bohemia. Auerbach studied music, but also developed a strong interest in photography. In 1939, when the Germans overran Bohemia, Erich Auerbach was forced to flee as a refugee and came to London where he worked for the Czechoslovak Government-in-Exile, from April 1941 until July 1945. After the war he worked in London for the weekly magazine *Illustrated*, until it closed down in 1957. He then worked as a freelance photographer. His photographs were exhibited in Prague Castle in May 2005.

Information courtesy of MONICA BEAUMONT

68. Erich Auerbach
Erich Auerbach took photographs of Beneš's official trips, events and meetings with armed forces. He took a series of official pictures at Aston Abbotts on 10th October 1944.

Courtesy of MONICA BEAUMONT

69. Business Card
Erich Auerbach's business card.

Courtesy of MONICA BEAUMONT

70. In the office
Erich Auerbach at his office in the Department of Information, London. As well as taking photographs, Erich Auerbach also wrote captions and designed book covers.

Film still courtesy of MONICA BEAUMONT

71. Working at home

Text on photo: *"Pozdrav z (Greetings from) Aston Abbotts"*.
President Beneš wrote his speeches and political books at
Aston Abbotts. Many of these were published in English
by the Czechoslovak Government-in-Exile in London, and
after the war were printed in Czech in Prague.

Signed photograph taken 1944 courtesy of MIROSLAV SMUTNÝ

72. Relaxing at home

Original caption:

*"An 'at home' picture showing the President of the Czechoslovak Republic,
Madam Hana Benešová and their Alsatian, Toga."*
Mrs Beneš is inspecting a book of photographs about the life of her husband,
Edvard Beneš (note 'EB' on the front cover).

Photo and caption by ERICH AUERBACH, 1944

73. Mrs Hana Beneš (1885-1974)

Text with photo: "z *(from)* Aston Abbotts"

Mrs Hana Beneš was Honorary President of the Czechoslovak Red Cross. She had an office on the floor above her husband's at 9 Grosvenor Place, London.

Signed photograph 20th February 1941, courtesy of MIROSLAV SMUTNÝ

74. Tea for ladies

Mrs Hana Beneš *(centre)* holding a party in the garden of The Abbey at Aston Abbotts, for President Beneš's 60th birthday on 28th May 1944. To the left of Mrs Beneš is Miss Jiřina Beneš, President Beneš's niece. With them are female officials of the Czechoslovak Government in Exile, the wives of the Chancellery officials from Wingrave, and the wives of the Military Intelligence staff from Addington.

Photograph courtesy of the MASARYK INSTITUTE, Prague

75. Herbert Revilliod (1921-1945)

Herbert Revilliod was Jan Masaryk's nephew and he was a gifted musician. He is shown here playing the violin by the croquet lawn at Aston Abbotts. On 13th February 1945 he died of tuberculosis in Edinburgh, Scotland.

76. Leonard Revilliod (1922-1944)

Leonard Revilliod was a flying officer in the RAF 518 Squadron. He is shown here out for a walk with President Beneš and Toga the dog. Leonard was killed in a flying accident off the coast of Scotland on 16th August 1944.

77. Ludmila Lipová (1890-1983)

Mrs Beneš walking with Ludmila Lipová and Toga along Lines Hill between Aston Abbotts and Weedon. Ludmila Lipová was the daughter of Ludvík Masaryk (1854-1912), Jan Masaryk's uncle.

THE MASARYK FAMILY IN ENGLAND

Herbert & Leonard Revilliod, children of Jan Masaryk's younger sister Olga Revilliod (1891-1978), were the only grandsons of Tomáš Masaryk. Jan Masaryk's older sister Alice Masaryk (1879-1966) worked for the Czechoslovak Red Cross in London.

78. The Beneš's nieces

Left to right: Mrs Božena Klučka, Mrs Gerke and Miss Jiřina Beneš. Dr and Mrs Beneš had no children of their own. They lived with two nieces, Mrs Božena Klučka (1904-1982) and Miss Jiřina Beneš (1909-1963), who acted as housekeepers, and secretaries for Mrs Beneš. Mrs Gerke worked for Jan Masaryk and was a visitor to Aston Abbotts.

Courtesy of the MASARYK INSTITUTE, Prague. Information courtesy of MIROSLAV SMUTNÝ

79. The croquet lawn

Dr Beneš is playing croquet with his niece Miss Jiřina Beneš in the grounds of The Abbey. The Abbey had a large lawn where the Beneš family would play croquet with their guests.

Courtesy of MICHAL KOLÁŘ

STAFF OF THE ABBEY HOUSEHOLD

The Beneš household employed a butler Mr Lumir Krob, a maid Miss Vilemina (Vilma) Kulhánek, a chauffeur Mr Syd Byatt, an English teacher Miss Thomas and a cook Miss Jana Čvančar, who married Jan Šnicer, one of the guards, in 1941. Mr & Mrs Šnicer later emigrated to the USA.

THE BRITISH CIVILIAN HOME GUARD

The national Home Guard was formed on 14th May 1940 as the Local Defence Volunteers, to protect the Home Front in the event of invasion.
Commander of "C" Company of the 1st Buckinghamshire Battalion was Major Harold Morton of The Old House, Aston Abbotts.
The Aston Abbotts Platoon was under the command of Lieutenant Albert Williams (1895-1964) of The Cottage, The Abbey, Aston Abbotts.
The Wingrave Platoon was under the command of Lieutenant Ralph Higgins (1888-1947) of Windmill Hill Farm, Wingrave.

obverse   reverse

obverse   reverse

80. Cyril John Simmons (1896-1944)

Sergeant Cyril John Simmons of Aston Abbotts in his Home Guard uniform.
The Home Guard was formed from civilian recruits between the ages of 17 and 65.
It was stood down on 3rd December 1944.

Courtesy of PETER KENT

81. Defence Medal – 1945

Home Guard Defence Medals were given to members of the British Home Guard on behalf of King George VI on 16th August 1945. The Home Guard was disbanded on 31st December 1945.

Courtesy of PETER KENT

82. Czechoslovak Medal of Merit – 1947

In January 1947, Lieutenant R. P. Higgins was awarded the Czechoslovak Republic's (Č.S.R) Medal for Merit (za zásluhy) First Class for his services to the protection of the Czechoslovak officials in Wingrave.

Photograph from author's collection

83 Defensive Log – wheel
Freda, Olive and Muriel Jennings.

84. Defensive Log
Robert Parrin and Freda Jennings.

85. Defensive Log – Stump pivot
Ron and Olive Jennings.

HOME GUARD DEFENSIVE LOGS, WINGRAVE ROAD, ASTON ABBOTTS
During the war, Aston Abbotts and Wingrave had defensive barriers made from elm tree logs. The logs were pivoted at one end, and could be swung round on a wheel. At Aston Abbotts there were three such logs on each of the roads into the village. Photos taken June 1942, courtesy of RON JENNINGS

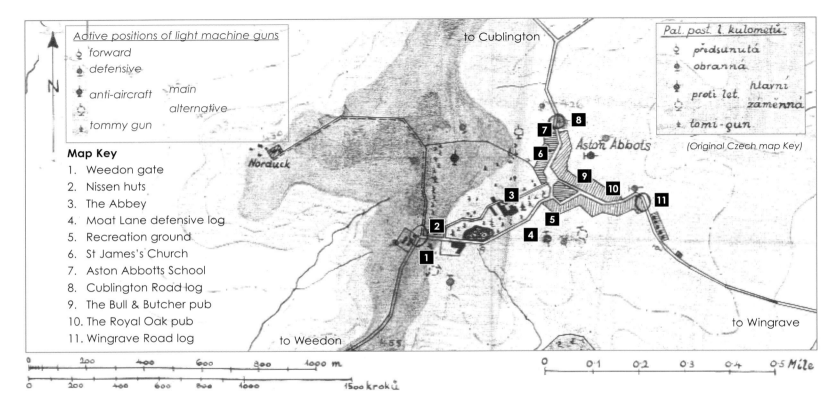

Active positions of light machine guns
- forward
- defensive
- anti-aircraft
- main
- alternative
- tommy gun

Map Key
1. Weedon gate
2. Nissen huts
3. The Abbey
4. Moat Lane defensive log
5. Recreation ground
6. St James's Church
7. Aston Abbotts School
8. Cublington Road log
9. The Bull & Butcher pub
10. The Royal Oak pub
11. Wingrave Road log

to Cublington

Norduck

Aston Abbots

Pal. post. l. kulometů:
- předsunutá
- obranná
- proti let. hlavní zaměnná
- tomi-gun

(Original Czech map Key)

to Wingrave

to Weedon

0 200 400 600 800 1000 m

0 200 400 600 800 1000 1500 kroků

0 0·1 0·2 0·3 0·4 0·5 Míle

86. Military map of Aston Abbotts

A platoon of the Czechoslovak army was based at Aston Abbotts for the protection of the President and his household. On this original Czech military map of Aston Abbotts, the forward and defensive active positions are shown for light machine guns, main and alternative anti-aircraft gun positions and tommy guns. These guns were based at different locations around Aston Abbotts. The map scales are shown in metres (m), paces (kroků) and miles. The Czechoslovak guards also operated the three Home Guard defensive logs.

Courtesy of the MILITARY ARCHIVE, Prague. Assistance with Czech translations courtesy of JAN HYRMAN and COL. PETR MILLER

1. Corporal Adolf Sheffel
2. Lance Corporal Vojta Levín
3. Private Arnošt Tscherney

87. Briefing soldiers at Aston Abbotts

President Beneš briefing a new group of guards, from the Second Company of the Second Infantry Battalion based at Walton Hall, Wellesbourne, Warwickshire. They have recently arrived in Aston Abbotts, and are carrying their gas masks. President Beneš is explaining their duties and the need to be alert for possible German parachutists. They are under the command of Lieutenant Rudolf Hanák.

Photograph taken in early 1941, courtesy of the MILITARY ARCHIVE, Prague. Identifications courtesy of VOJTA LEVÍN

88. Czechoslovak badge

This Czechoslovak badge was given as a souvenir to Lieutenant Ralph Higgins of the Wingrave Home Guard.

89. Infantry Battalion Badge

The badge of the 2nd Infantry Battalion (pěší pluk), of the Czechoslovak Army. The Battalion was founded in 1940 at Agde, near Béziers, in the south of France.

90. The permanent presidential guards at Aston Abbotts, 1940-1945

In October 1940, the British War Office agreed that President Beneš could have a permanent guard of 14 soldiers for his security. They were selected from the Czechoslovak Army, which from 13th October 1940 to 15th May 1942 was based in locations near Leamington Spa, Warwickshire. In this photo, the guards offer President Beneš a traditional Czech greeting of bread and salt upon his first visit to the camp.

Courtesy of the MILITARY ARCHIVE, Prague. Photo taken November 1940

91. Tent encampment

From 1940 to 1942, each company of the Czechoslovak Army took it in turns to send volunteers as additional guards to Aston Abbotts on a three-week rotation. They lived in tents until Nissen huts were built.

Photograph taken December 1940, courtesy of the MILITARY ARCHIVE, Prague

92. Bedford truck arriving at Aston Abbotts

The guards from the Czechoslovak Army near Leamington Spa in Warwickshire arrived by Bedford Truck on Monday mornings.
After their three week stay they would be waved off by local children.
This truck was an MWD Light Utility Truck built by Bedford trucks, a division of Vauxhall Motors at nearby Luton, Bedfordshire.

Photo taken about 1941, courtesy of HILDA HARPER

93. Despatch rider

Each guard unit had its own despatch rider, who went 60 miles north to Leamington Spa each day to take post and get instructions and news from the main Czechoslovak Army.

This motorbike was an M20 model built by British Small Arms (BSA) at Small Heath, Birmingham.

Photo taken about 1941, courtesy of HILDA HARPER

94. Guard group at Aston Abbotts

A photo was taken each time a new group of guards arrived from Warwickshire. They usually had about 30 men including a cook, a despatch rider and a unit commander. In January 1941 this group worked with Italian prisoners of war from Princes Risborough, Bucks, to build Nissen huts, using supplies from the Army depot at High Wycombe, Bucks. Two of these Nissen huts still remain standing in the village.

Photograph courtesy of the MASARYK INSTITUTE, Prague. Information courtesy of VOJTA LEVÍN

95. Officers and Privates at Aston Abbotts

President Beneš *(centre)* with General Rudolf Viest beside him.

The soldiers *(back rows)* are the presidential guards from the 2nd Infantry Battalion, normally based at Walton Hall, near Leamington Spa.

The Officers *(front left)* are from the Czechoslovak Army, who have been meeting their British counterparts *(front right)*.

Photograph from author's collection. This is also the front cover image. Photograph taken 2nd July 1941 in the grounds of The Abbey

97. ABC
Insignia of the Aylesbury Brewery Company (ABC), showing the white Aylesbury duck. ABC supplied the beer to the pubs in the Aylesbury Vale. This brewery no longer trades.

THE PUBS TODAY
The Royal Oak is still a popular place for food and drink. In March 2003 the Bull & Butcher closed. It has since been converted into dwellings called Humphreys Close.

96. The Royal Oak pub, Aston Abbotts
The Royal Oak pub dates back to the 17th century. In the war it was run by Bill & Audrey Williams who served locals and Czechoslovak soldiers. Bill's sister Pamela Williams married a Czech soldier called Karel (known as Charles) Spálenka in 1944.

Drawing courtesy of ANDY BYSTRA. Information courtesy of VICTOR SCOTT

98. The Bull & Butcher pub, Aston Abbotts
The Bull & Butcher pub also included the village bakery. In the war it was run by Thomas and Christina Humphreys. It was very popular with the Czechoslovak guards, especially when they were on Home Guard duty. It was here that the Czechoslovaks learnt to play darts.

Drawing courtesy of ANDY BYSTRA. Information courtesy of FRANK HUMPHREYS

99. The cook

Every Tuesday and Thursday, the Czechoslovak guards' cook, Martin, used the baker's oven at the Bull & Butcher pub, where he could often be found drinking.

Courtesy of the MASARYK INSTITUTE, Prague

100. Supplies for the Czechoslovaks in Buckinghamshire

The guards kept their own black leghorn chickens at their encampment in Aston Abbotts. Rabbits and pigs were kept by the Czechoslovaks at Wingrave. The pigs were named after the three French collaborators: Petain, Darlan and Daladier. Supplies for the Czechoslovaks at Addington came from W. E. Illing's grocery shop in Winslow, Bucks. President Beneš's Cox's Orange Pippins and Russet apples came from the Holland's orchard at White House Farm at Shenley Church End, Bucks.

Courtesy of the MASARYK INSTITUTE, Prague. Information courtesy of MIROSLAV SMUTNÝ, DAVID ILLING and JEAN WELLCOME

101. The Bull's Head, Aylesbury

The Bull's Head was the favourite place to go for the guards stationed at Aston Abbotts. A Bedford truck known as "the liberty truck" would take those who were not on duty to Aylesbury each evening, stopping at the Bull's Head and then Aylesbury Station. It would leave Aylesbury Station at 10:30 p.m. stopping at the Bull's Head and then back to Aston Abbotts. Those missing the truck would have to walk home.

Courtesy of BUCKS COUNTY MUSEUM, Aylesbury. Information courtesy of VOJTA LEVÍN

102. Military parades in Buckinghamshire

The Czechoslovak soldiers at Aston Abbotts paraded in Aylesbury, Bucks for War Weapons Week on 19th April 1941; in Aylesbury for United Nations Day on Sunday 14th June 1942; and in High Wycombe, Bucks, for Salute the Soldier Week on 20th May 1944.

This photograph shows the 1942 United Nations parade in Market Square, Aylesbury, which was broadcast live on BBC Radio. The photograph includes British, American and Czechoslovak serviceman from around Buckinghamshire, behind the flags of the Allies.

Courtesy of BUCKS COUNTY MUSEUM, Aylesbury. Information from back issues of THE BUCKS HERALD

ENTERTAINMENT

The presidential guards organised fun evenings, especially on Czech and Slovak special days, such as St. Wenceslas Day (28 September) and St. Nicholas Day (6 December). They would invite the other guards, the household of The Abbey, and "the court" from Wingrave.

103. Theatre group

In this photograph the entertainment is provided in one of the Nissen huts by the 3rd company of the 1st Battalion from Moreton Paddox House, near Warwick. They were in Aston Abbotts from 20th November until 15th December 1941 under their Commanding Officer Miloslav Kašpar.

RUDOLF KRZÁK (1914-2004)

Second from the left at the back is 1st Lieutenant Rudolf Krzák, who was deputy commander of Special Group D, which with the SOE trained paratroopers for special operations, including Operation Anthropoid.

Information courtesy of GEN. M.F. KAŠPAR

Wishing you a happy Christmas and may the New Year lead on to Victory!

104. Christmas & New Year card
This card shows a tank in front of the arms of Czechoslovakia.

105. Card Greetings
Card sent from Vasil Hlinka on 13th December 1941

BACKGROUND TO THE CARDS
These photographs *(numbers 106 and 109)* were taken whilst the Czechoslovak Army was stationed in the grounds of Cholmondeley Castle, Cholmondeley, near Malpas, Cheshire, from July to October 1940. The Army then moved to Warwickshire until 1942, from where Corporals Hlinka and Chajdiak were sent on guard duty to Aston Abbotts. These cards were sent to Miss Hilda Humphreys at the Bull & Butcher pub after the guards returned to Moreton Hall, near Leamington Spa, in December 1941.

106. Corporal Vasil Hlinka

Wishing you all happiness this Christmas-tide, and may the sacrifices of the dying year lead on to the creation of the better world for which we are all fighting !

Štefan Ch.

107. Christmas & New Year card
This card shows a Czechoslovak soldier killing the Nazi dragon.

108. Card Greetings
Card sent from Štefan Chajdiak in December 1941.

109. Corporal Štefan Chajdiak

VILÉM TAUSKÝ (1910-2004)

In September 1939, Corporal Vilém Tauský was appointed Military Bandmaster and formed a military band. He formed the Czechoslovak Army Choir which sang throughout Britain. He wrote the score for a film, *Interim Balance* – the history of the Czechoslovak Army in exile. He arranged and conducted a farewell concert for President Beneš and his provisional Government prior to their departure for Prague. From 1956-1967 he conducted the BBC Concert Orchestra.

110. Czechoslovak Army Band

The Czechoslovak Army Band stayed in Aston Abbotts between February and March 1942. Conducting the band is Corporal Vilém Tauský.

111. Audience

Mr & Mrs Beneš with the Smutný family and Generals from Wingrave. They are being entertained by the presidential guards at Aston Abbotts.

Back row, left to right:
General Sergej Ingr[?];
General Rudolf Viest;
visiting Allied General;
Miss Ludmila Kašpařík
(Dr Smutný's Secretary);
General Antonín Hasal.

Front row, left to right:
local boy;
Miss Broomfield
(children's governess);
Miroslav Smutný
(youngest son of Dr & Mrs Smutný);
Mrs Jaroslava Smutný;
President Edvard Beneš;
Mrs Hana Beneš;
Dr Jaromír Smutný.

Photograph taken about 1944 at Aston Abbotts.

Courtesy of the MASARYK INSTITUTE, Prague.

Identifications courtesy of MIROSLAV SMUTNÝ

112. Officer and guards

Members of the permanent presidential guard at Aston Abbotts, who lived in the Nissen huts behind Abbey Cottages, Moat Lane, Aston Abbotts. Second from the left is Lieutenant Cyril Novák and on the far right is Sergeant Jan Krčma, who was known as John.

Courtesy of the MASARYK INSTITUTE, Prague. Information courtesy of BARBARA PERRY

113. Smutný talks to the guards

The chief of President Beneš's officials, Dr Jaromír Smutný, talks to the Czechoslovak guards visiting from the Leamington Spa area. Dr Smutný was visiting President Beneš from his home in Wingrave. Behind the group is one of the Nissen huts, which still stands today.

Courtesy of the MASARYK INSTITUTE, Prague

DAILY LIFE OF A PRESIDENTIAL GUARD

Czechoslovak soldiers earnt a daily pay of 2/6d (12½ pence) and a 5d clothing allowance.

They had a daily newspaper called Naše noviny (Our News), which was printed in Leamington Spa and edited by Václav Straka.

At Aston Abbotts their post was delivered by Bernard Osborn, who afterwards drank coffee with the Czechoslovak guards.

Information courtesy of JIŘÍ PAVEL, VÁCLAV STRAKA and BERNARD OSBORN

115. Guards

The presidential bodyguards at Aston Abbotts. Jan (known as John) is holding their pet cat *"Kočka"* ("Cat"), who was the camp mascot. Behind them are wooden huts which were demolished in 1945.

Photo courtesy of the MASARYK INSTITUTE, Prague. Information courtesy of VICTOR SCOTT

114. Czechoslovak medal

This commemorative medal was awarded in October 1943, for service in Great Britain (*Velká Britanie*). A strip above the guards' left pocket represented its award.

Courtesy of ECKART DISSEN

SPORT

Fitness was important in the Czechoslovak Army. At Aston Abbotts, the soldiers had a volleyball court, a tennis court and a football pitch. The Czechoslovak Army also had a football team called the Carpathians, which once played the London Brick Company (LBC) at Bletchley.

Information courtesy of VICTOR SCOTT, BARBARA PERRY, ROY TINK and JOSEF KALAŠ

116. Private's cap badge

This badge was worn by Privates on their caps, as shown in these photographs. The badge displays the heraldic lion of Bohemia bearing the shield of Slovakia.

Courtesy of HILDA HARPER

Photo taken about 1941 courtesy of MRS MARY PAVEZKA

117. Officer's badge

Czechoslovak cap badge worn by officers. This was based on the British design, but has the heraldic device of Czechoslovakia on a diamond with two swords behind.

Courtesy of HILDA HARPER

118. Vladimír Pavezka (1914-2001)

2nd Lieutenant Vladimír Pavezka was President Beneš's bodyguard at Aston Abbotts between 1st October 1943 and 15th March 1944.

From his unpublished memoirs written in 2001:

"I was given the job of accompanying Beneš when he carried out various official duties and it was during the nine months I spent with him that I met a number of the notables of the time, including several heads of state, when they visited Aston Abbotts, and on one occasion Winston Churchill himself."

ALLIED LEADERS AT ASTON ABBOTTS

Exiled Allied leaders who visited Beneš at Aston Abbotts included: King Haakon VII of Norway (1872-1957); Queen Wilhelmina of the Netherlands (1880-1962); Charles de Gaulle of Free France (1890-1970) who was based nearby at Asheridge Park, Hertfordshire; and General Władysław Sikorski of Poland (1881-1943) who was based at Iver, Bucks.

119. Slovak delegation, October 1944

Left to right: President Beneš; Ladislav 'Laco' Novomeský (1904-1976) of the Communist Party; Ján Ursíny (1896-1972) of the Democratic Party; and Lt. Col. Vencl. The delegation are visiting Aston Abbotts from the Slovak National Council in Bratislava, Slovakia. They presented President Beneš with a commemorative walking stick. The Slovak delegation were in England to discuss the Slovak Uprising and the liberation.

Courtesy of the MASARYK INSTITUTE, Prague

120. Slovak state symbol

This shows a white double cross on a red background on three blue mountains.

SLOVAKIA

Slovakia had declared independence on 14th March 1939 and was assisted by Nazi Germany. On 29th August 1944 the Slovak Uprising against the Germans began. Slovakia was re-incorporated into Czechoslovakia in 1945. The Czech and Slovak Republics split up again on 1st January 1993.

> 9, GROSVENOR PLACE,
> LONDON, S.W. 1.
>
> SLOANE 8105.
>
> 28th February 1945.
>
> Dear Victor,
>
> My husband was very pleased with your letter and its good wishes, and asks me to send you this little book with his greetings. We are so glad to know that you are interested in our country, and hope you may visit it one day.
>
> I wonder if you still remember the Czech you have learnt. It was so pleasant to hear you greet us in our own language.
>
> We shall often think of Aston Abbotts with pleasure, when we are home again.
>
> With all good wishes,
>
> *yours sincerely*
>
> *Hana Benešová*
>
> /Madame Edvard Beneš/

121. Farewell letter, 28th February 1945

A letter written by Mrs Hana Beneš. It was written in reply to a letter from Victor Scott of Aston Abbotts, sending them best wishes for their return home.

After the war Victor Scott visited Dr and Mrs Beneš at Hradčany Castle in Prague.

Courtesy of VICTOR SCOTT

122. Leaving Buckinghamshire, 10th March 1945

Last picture of the Czechoslovaks at The Abbey in Aston Abbotts.
Left to right: Lieutenant Colonel Cyril Novák, commander of the presidential guard; President Beneš; General Oldřich Španiel; Dr Jaromír Smutný; Mrs Beneš; Mrs Božena Klučka and Miss Jiřina Beneš, the President's nieces; Toga the Alsatian; and Dr Oskar Klinger (1898-1973), personal doctor to President Beneš and Jan Masaryk. The Abbey was handed back to the Mortons on Saturday March 17th 1945, when the last of Dr. Beneš's staff left the building.

Courtesy of the MASARYK INSTITUTE, Prague

S.R.—L.N.E.R.

LONDON
Victoria Street
TO
PRAGUE
Masaryk Street

Available for three
month from date of
issue.

FIRST
for conditions see back
019440

actual size

123. Leaving England, 11th March 1945

Jan Masaryk *(left)*, President Edvard Beneš *(in front of the microphone)*, and Mrs Hana Beneš *(right)* about to board an aeroplane to leave England. The Government-in-Exile flew to Moscow in three RAF bombers to attend talks with Stalin, before entering the liberated territories of Czechoslovakia with the Red Army. On 4th April 1945 temporary Czechoslovak government headquarters were set up in Košice in Slovakia before moving to Prague on 16th and 17th May 1945. The wives and children of the Czechoslovak Government officials from London and Wingrave, were flown to Prague by the RAF from RAF Northolt in July 1945.

Photo by ERICH AUERBACH

124. Train ticket

First class ticket dated December 1944. Many of the Czechoslovaks returned home by train in summer 1945. This ticket was never used as it was only valid for 3 months. Liberation did not come in time.

Courtesy of MONICA BEAUMONT

125. School globe

This globe was given to Mrs L. Brock, headmistress of Aston Abbotts School, by Dr and Mrs Beneš as a Christmas present on 24th December 1942.

Photos taken by PIERS PETTMAN in 2004 courtesy of BUCKS COUNTY MUSEUM, Aylesbury

126. Wartime Europe

Close-up of the globe, showing Britain and Czechoslovakia in pre-war Europe.

> This Globe was presented to this School on the 24th. December, 1942, by Dr. Benes, late President of Czechoslovakia. He resided at the Abbey during the 1939-45 war.

127. Globe label

This label was put on the globe after the war.

128. Aston Abbotts Primary School, Cublington Road

During the war the school had 108 pupils from
Aston Abbotts, Cublington and London evacuees.
The school closed in 1972. It is now a private house.

Photo by PIERS PETTMAN, 2004. Information courtesy of VALERIE OSBORN

129. & 130. School climbing frame

Dr Beneš left the school managers £100 for the benefit of Aston Abbotts School.
After the war this money paid for a climbing frame, which was erected in the school
grounds. This was moved to the village recreation ground when the school closed.

Photos by NEIL REES, 2004

This bus shelter was donated by
President Benes of Czechoslovakia
to thank the people of
Aston Abbotts & Wingrave
whilst he and his cabinet were in
exile here during World War II

132. Shelter Plaque

The bus shelter plaque was
first proposed in 1948, but one
was not put up until 1992.

Photo by NEIL REES, 2004

OPENING CEREMONY

In September 1943 President Beneš
gave Wingrave Parish Council
£150 to build a bus shelter.
A ceremony was held on Saturday
15th April 1944 when the bus
shelter was formally handed over
by Jaromír Smutný on behalf of
President Beneš. The ceremony
was attended by representatives
from Aston Abbotts and Wingrave.
At the end they gave three cheers
for President Beneš.

131. Bus Shelter

The bus shelter on the A418 between Aylesbury and Leighton Buzzard, was given to the villages of
Aston Abbotts and Wingrave by President Beneš in 1944. People from Wingrave and Aston Abbotts
travelling to Aylesbury would wait for the bus at the Crossroads, midway between Aston Abbotts and
Wingrave. The bus shelter was built by Messrs Fleet & Roberts of Wingrave, and was kept clean by
Archibald "Roadman" Gurnett (1884-1961) of Wingrave. The bus shelter is still used today.

Photo taken 2005 by BOB McLEOD. Information courtesy of PRUDENCE GOODWIN and PETER KENT

133. V. E. Day tile, 1945

A Czechoslovak ceramic tile commemorating the liberation of Prague by the Red Army on 9th May 1945. It shows the Town Hall in Prague, with Czech symbols. After the war the tile was given to Mrs Humphreys at the Bull & Butcher in Aston Abbotts. Dr Beneš was re-elected as President on the 26th May 1945.

134. Letter from Prague, 1947

In 1945 there were about 600 British war brides in Czechoslovakia, including Mrs Pamela Spálenka of Aston Abbotts. Contact was maintained between people in Aston Abbotts and their friends in Czechoslovakia until 1948. Then the Czechoslovak soldiers who had been in Britain, were either imprisoned by the communist authorities or escaped into exile again.

obverse: Jan Masaryk   *reverse: In Memoriam   10-III-1948*

actual size

135. Jan Masaryk Memorial Medallion

On 10th March 1948, Jan Masaryk was found dead in mysterious circumstances below the window of his second-storey flat at the Ministry of Foreign Affairs in Prague. He was 61 years of age. The official verdict by the communist authorities was suicide, but in January 2004 the Czech police closed the case with an official verdict of murder. He is buried with his parents and sister, Alice Masaryk, at Lány in Bohemia. His sister Olga Masaryk Revilliod died in Farnham Royal, Bucks on 12th September 1978, aged 87.

Author's collection

136. Edvard Beneš Memorial Medallion

President Beneš resigned on 7th June 1948. He had previously suffered from heart attacks in England and Czechoslovakia, and he died of ill health on 3rd September 1948 aged 64. He is buried in the grounds of his private villa in Sezimovo Ústí, near Tábor in Bohemia. Mrs Hana Beneš continued to live in Sezimovo Ústí and Prague until she died on 2nd December 1974, aged 89.

Courtesy of CYNTHIA KENT

BIBLIOGRAPHY

**Útěk do druhého odboje
(Escape to the Second Resistance)**
by Josef Hodek
Josef Hodek was one of the permanent presidential bodyguards at Aston Abbotts. This book gives a first-hand account of life at Aston Abbotts.

Published in Czech only

**Master of Spies – The Memoirs of General Moravec /
Špión jemuž nevěřili**
by Colonel František Moravec
This book gives a first-hand account of the work of the military intelligence and the move from London to Addington, Bucks.

Published in English & Czech

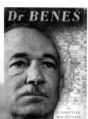

Dr Beneš
by Compton MacKenzie
Compton MacKenzie (1883-1972) spent many hours interviewing Dr Beneš at Aston Abbotts using a stenograph, staying at the King's Head in Aylesbury. He was assisted by Josef Löwenbach at Wingrave.

Published in English & Czech

Edvard Beneš: Rozpravy a úvahy věnované presidentu Dr Edvardu Benešovi k jeho šedasátým narozeninám / Edward Beneš: Essays and Reflections Presented on the Occasion of His Sixtieth Birthday
edited by Jan Opočenský (1885-1961), Beneš's archivist
This is a collection of essays by statesmen about Beneš.

Published in English & Czech

**Pan President se nám vrátil
(Mr President returns to us)**
by Eduard Táborský
Eduard Táborský was President Beneš's private secretary and this book includes a first-hand account of President Beneš working at Aston Abbotts.

Published in Czech only

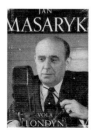

Volá Londýn / Speaking to My Country
by Jan Masaryk
This book has transcripts of Jan Masaryk's BBC radio speeches, broadcast from London to Czechoslovakia between 8th October 1939 and 5th August 1945.

Published in English & Czech

ACKNOWLEDGEMENTS

Primary Sources of information

This book has been compiled using conversations and correspondence with people and families of people who were part of the story:

■ FRIENDS OF JAN MASARYK
Renée Robeson, Jean Wellcome

■ PEOPLE OF ADDINGTON
Margaret Crook, David Crook, Elizabeth Calcutt, Bob Dickens, Mary Cheshire, David Illing, Cyril Corbett, Bob Hart

■ PEOPLE OF ASTON ABBOTTS
Hilda Harper, Frank Humphreys, Colin Higgs, Natalie Higgs, Victor Scott, Bernard Osborn, Valerie Osborn, Peter Kent, Ron Jennings, Freda Gregory, George Brandon, Barbara Perry, Wilfred Halsey

■ PEOPLE OF WINGRAVE
Cherry-Anne Evans, Peggy Hewitt, Prudence Goodwin, Jean Rogers, Norman Brackley, Arthur Bandy, George Tighe

■ HOCKLIFFE RADIO STATION
Roy Tink, Jiří Louda, George Bearfield and the family of Jaroslav Bublík, Joy Square, D. W. Room

■ ASTON ABBOTTS PRESIDENTIAL GUARDS
General Miloslav Kašpar, Vojtěch Levín,
Mrs Mary Pavezka and the family of Vladimír Pavezka

■ CZECHOSLOVAK GOVERNMENT-IN-EXILE
Hana Ludikar and the family of Ladislav Feierabend,
Monica Beaumont and the family of Erich Auerbach, Miroslav Smutný

Assistance

I have also had the assistance of many people:

■ BUCKINGHAMSHIRE & BEDFORDSHIRE
Piers Pettman, Kirsty Crombie Smith, Bob McLeod, Peter & Clare Shorrock, Jeff & Mandy Banister, Kate Curry, Steve Holdsworth, Patrick House, Ann Bailey, Robert Ayers, Andy Bystra, David Critchley, John Taylor, Shirley Ford, Dickie Dickins, John Pether, David White, A. Wise, Geoff Bond, Geoff Aldridge; Jean Yates, Philip Maxey

■ LEAMINGTON SPA, WARWICKSHIRE
Alan Griffin, cousin Elaine Barker, Jiří Pavel, Josef Kalaš

■ CZECH EMBASSY, LONDON
Colonel Petr Miller, Monika Studená, Ambassador Štefan Füle

■ HISTORICAL CONSULTANTS, ENGLAND
Jan Kaplan, Martin Brown, Maria Dowling, Mark Cornwall, Geoffrey Pidgeon, Pat Hawker, John Gallehawk

■ CZECH REPUBLIC
Dagmar Hájková, Michal Kolář, Jan Hyrman, Joy Kadečková, Toni Špaček, Václav Straka, Pavel Vlček, Tomáš Bernhardt, Tomáš Hájek

■ ARCHIVES & LIBRARIES
Masaryk Institute, Prague; the Military Archive of Prague; National Film Archive, Prague; National Archives, Kew; County Record Office, Aylesbury; Bucks County Museum, Aylesbury; Buckingham Library; Leamington Spa Library

■ TRANSLATION, PRODUCTION & PROOF READING
Diana Rosová; Peter Hawkes; Jessica Schilling, Frances Russell, Margaret Rees, Elspeth Crombie Smith, Richard Beith

Disclaimer: In all matters I have tried to be accurate and correct. If you know of any errors or omissions please contact me and these will be corrected in the next edition of the book. NEIL REES